Our Little Agonies

Jen Colclough

Montreal Publishing Company

Cover Art by Jen Colclough

1st Edition, May 1, 2025

ISBN: 978-1-998353-08-8

Montreal Publishing Company

Dedicated to:

David and Rose Raftus
Memorabo vos.

Introduction

C ontrary to its title, this collection of poems is not tragic. It is, however, composed by a historian, so you'll have to forgive the scar tissue. Please know that I've taken pains to lace these poems with a considerable amount of strategic hope.

Hopefulness is not a trait typically attributed to historians. This is likely due to the rather heavy-handed adage that history is 'doomed' to repeat itself. *How cynical!* If you have ever found yourself uttering this phrase in defeat, then I have some excellent news for you: If history seems to be repeating itself, this also means that it continues. That *we* continue. The historian's attempt to draw connection between otherwise disparate moments in space and time is therefore a supremely hopeful and human act.

In many ways, historians and poets share the same purpose: to seek out evidence of humanity and, in its absence, to create it.

Both fields are fluent in the language of absence. Consider, for example, the abundance of broken statuary. In the halls of grand museums, dowel rods protrude from chests and arms where the marble is too fragile to bear its own weight. Arms are snapped off like twigs and legs are missing. The delicate folds of stone garments are preserved while noses are not, making aesthetic the dominant feature, not identity.

The flaws of ancient stone endear them to us. Historians and museum patrons alike value the statues even more for their impossibility. One look at the fragmented marble and we count ourselves lucky that we have any piece of it at all. When we study the past, we become allies and advocates of absence as we deftly maneuver around the craters.

As a Classical historian, I am trained in a field built on the premise that the pieces are enough. That the echoes of the past resound loudly enough for us to recognize, relish, and celebrate those distant moments. In a field that stacks theory upon uncertain theory, brokenness is a prerequisite.

So, no; this book is not a celebration of tragedy but an ode to endurance— to the pieces left behind.

Some years have teeth; I will not pretend otherwise. It was during the pandemic, when family members grappled with illness, dementia, and depression, that my poetic practice became a navigational tool. Given my historical background, I am (thankfully) incapable of forging a path forward without facing the past. Armed with Faulkner's conviction that the past is never over, I befriended the ghosts I'd studied. Aeneas, Dante, and Virgil are scattered throughout these pages as they claw their way forward on their respective journeys.

In quarantine, I thought often of Aeneas, who did not have time to grieve his wife and father because of his duty. In fact, the gods had to repeatedly urge Aeneas to set aside tears in order to pursue the greater task of founding a city. Rome needed to exist not as a burial place for the dead but to ensure that the living—the survivors of Troy—would have a homeland. In an almost unbearably human act, Aeneas was forced to build a refuge from the ruins even as he crawled out of them.

And then, there was Dante.

While attending an interdisciplinary Classics conference hosted by the University of Toronto, a lecture on Virgil's role in Dante's *Inferno* triggered a realization. As I witnessed family members grappling with dementia, I understood with renewed urgency Dante's choice to be guided through *Inferno* by his favourite, long-dead poet.

We all need a guide. When we cannot find one, we use the tools at our disposal to forge a new one. To summon a guardian from the ancient past is to believe that such acute pain has been endured before, perhaps even by our heroes. There it is again—that historical optimism. The insistence upon a thread.

I believe the poet's duty is much the same as the historian's—to seek connection, to tell the truth, and to admit that absence is everywhere, but so is memory.

In these pages, you will find snapshots of Dante, Virgil, and Aeneas on their journeys. Their evolution throughout the work communicates a progression as well as a conviction: The night is dark, but it will end.

As you read on, I invite you to imagine me serenading the craters as I step over them, remembering.

Acknowledgements

Several of the poems in this collection have been featured previously in other magazines and collections.

"Astronautica," was longlisted by the *League of Canadian Poets* for their annual "Summer Lovin' Contest."

"Haiku #1," first appeared in *Porch to Porch: A Maritime Haiku Anthology*.

"Miasma," "May," and "Sleeping on My Best Friend's Couch," appeared in Volume IV of the *Not Ghosts, But Spirits Anthology*.

"Dies Irae," appeared in *Tabula Rasa Review* in June 2024.

"The King of Grief," was published in Issue 6 of *The Heimat Review*.

"Untranslatable/Unübersetzbar" and "Connoisseurs of Lightness," appeared in the inaugural issue of *ionosphere*. "Connoisseurs of Lightness" was nominated for the Pushcart Prize in 2024.

"Ithaca," was published in the Autumn 2023 Issue of *Open Door Magazine*.

"Gabriel," appeared in *MORIA Literary Magazine* and was later reprinted in *The Forgotten Fragments of Time Anthology*.

"May," and "Συγγράφεια," were featured in the August 2023 edition of *Tidewise Illustrated Quarterly*.

In July 2023, "Futures," was published in *The Power of Hope Anthology*.

"Deep August," was featured in Issue 2 of *Free the Verse*.

"Plato Longs for Us," appeared in the *Opal Age Tribune* in 2024.

Finally, "Aeneas," was longlisted for the Classical Association's 2024 Poetry Competition.

Thank you to Mercey LePage, Derek Stephenson, Cara Morgan, and Janci Despain for your kind and thoughtful edits.

I cannot publish anything without thanking Meagan Cleveland, for her invaluable feedback, and for always replying when I send her quotes and poems, normally at inhumane hours.

Several of the poems in this collection were written in 2024 when I held the Shannon Residency at Beinn Mhàbu in Cape Breton, Nova Scotia. I am grateful to Beinn Mhàbu for supporting my creative work, and would like to thank the staff, students, and community members I met during that period for inviting me into their welcoming community. *Tapadh leibh.*

And finally, thank you to my family for enduring 'the writer in the attic.'

Contents

Part 1

«Or discendiam qua giù nel cieco mondo»,
Cominciò il poeta tutto smorto.
«Io sarò primo, e tu sarai secondo».

"Into the blind world let us now descend,"
Began the poet, his face as pale as death.
"I will go first, and you will follow me."

Inferno, Canto IV, trans. Anthony Esolen, lines 13-15

Canto 1

ABANDON ALL HOPE YOU WHO ENTER HERE.

The man made of Time
is waiting in his laurels
for me to move on. It is dark.
The night is not full of shadows
so much as it is full of ghosts.

> *Do not be afraid.*
> *Ghosts are nothing more than*
> *the atmosphere remembering*
> *itself.*

I, the still-living,
am more than a memory,
at least.
I press my ear against the door of the universe,
listening.

Do you hear anything?

My own breathing.

There is an inclination towards flight.
The dexterity of small birds in the face
of anything at all.
The Teacher
holds autumn in his mouth.
His voice rustles with dead leaves;
the more he speaks,
the less of him is left.

Figliuol mio,
come along.

The Teacher
does not know why
the sinners know my name
or that my faith is pledged
to the first hand that touches it.

There is much more to see,
says the man with no eyes.

He gave up looking long ago;
now he only knows.

Astronautica

You know by now that it is impolite to stand in the sun
just to ask where all the light is coming from.
Stand up, now. This is not your grave.
When you were a child, you mistook the moon
for an eyelet on God's shoe,
then held up a shoelace and dreamed
of threading it through the universe.
You begged your mother for those black converse with
    rainbow stars
so you could tread upon the sky the way God
treads upon the earth, touching only the idea of it.

    Aren't you tired of intangibility?
    Of gusting so violently that men erect crisp white sails
    just to profit from your path?

Remember, *astronaut* is Latin for *star-sailor,*
and you were the child with astrological feet and the desire
to weave the universe together,

to fasten God's shoe to the earth so that They would be
    there
to feel our tiny bodies like grains of sand, or milky stars,
crushed beneath the weight of our idea of Them,
but also to make every moment holy.

It is significant that you saw a celestial rock
and mistook it for an entry-point.
You, who tends to fall in love with those
who carry midnight on their backs just to see if
they can carry it.
    In the Bible,
angels are repeatedly uttering:
    Be not afraid! Be not afraid!
to those who beg for Intervention
but cannot meet its eyes.
In this, the commonest of eras,
you subscribe to a wider mercy.

Daffodils, violets, marigolds, and maze—
you touch them all with the pads of your thumbs, mut-
    tering:
    Be not afraid, be not afraid,
to the universe because you are not a shoe to crush
or a wind to be harnessed,

but an Observer who saw a light and mistook it for an
    invitation
for closeness.

Dies Irae

I.

"It's snowing," I tell you, but what I really mean is: *The world is shifting right now—come and see.* Outside, the windowsill is weighted down like the years, and the house is hunchbacked, cloaked in a white cardigan. "So it is," you say, and rebutton your own cardigan, the threadbare blue-black with a hole in the right-hand pocket. Everything of value goes in the left, now, and no one goes very far. It is January, and the year is beyond saving. We look out the windows, ignoring the door. To a flightless bird, all cages look the same.

II.

The seasonal translation of the earth will always be of
   interest to
those who tread upon it.

III.

The gardener insists it is necessary to cut away the rot. To
   consider

the benefits of amputation.

Looming over the workbench,

I consider also

the tremor

   of your voice just afterward,

   all severed

   into

   bits.

IV.

Sometimes the crater predates the cataclysm.

Sometimes grief insists upon itself.

V.

Cobalt, pearl,

   Cobalt, pearl.

   There are stripes

   where this wallpaper forgot

   to repeat itself.

   I make soup on the stove

   because it is cold.

   The blue-and-white carnations curve away from it,

recoiling.

The bowl

    waits on the stove all afternoon

    while you and I sit around it.

    Some things aren't destined for consumption alone.

VI.

My ivy plant died twice.

                It's no matter. So did I.

VII.

    There is a bridge behind my house that sometimes forgets to be a bridge. The heap of planks and nails that guards the stream spends all year waiting to be covered by a great white hand. Snow does not fall upon the bridge so much as it adorns it. All the best altars are accidental.

Each fresh snow makes me wonder
how your cardigan is holding up.

VIII.

That winter,
all the dawns were behind us
    and we knew it.

The Arsonist

Mine is not a story of return.
You will find no thresholds here.

When the house caught fire
I tried to put it out.
To sprinkle sand
when I could have salted the earth.
To call her name
when I could have called for help.
On the other side of ruin,
I kept my hands clean.
I waited for the smoke to pass.
Becoming a psychic requires more effort
than falling in love with an arsonist,
but the result is much the same.
In both cases, you know
how your love will end.
One night, I walked so far,

the future followed me there.
The house was tired and overgrown.
Old ash now haunted the furniture as dust.

   "Hello,"
   I told her forgotten shade, more silhouette than morn-
ing air,
   "What do you regret more? Striking the match?
   Or meeting me?"

Her eyelids blinked over empty sockets—
the lowering and raising of a portcullis.
The Arsonist did not answer.
When the house went up, it took her tongue with it.
She used to insist that we were safe.
That the house was sturdy,
its foundations sound.
What she meant was this:
   I can out run you. We are both safe
   so long as I can out run you.

Mine is not a story of return but returning.
All that's left is forward movement.
(And my bones,
still unburied in the backyard.)
I bequeath them to the animals and

archaeologists-

all those who love to play among the dirt.

House or prairie fire, the pattern is the same.

Fire first. Everything after.

When my heels strike the earth,

they leave no mark;

no one gets to see this part.

The part where Orpheus becomes Eurydice,

his own un-tragic wife,

following in her own footsteps.

Halfway to Morning

Look—
 a gate

                between two trees,
    pretending to be a door.

    Snowflakes fall sideways,
    knocking.

    I used to think of home
    as the sound of my name being called from the next
room,
                forever.
    Or a mistranslation of her name
                called again,
                and again,
                and again.

    I watch as you take another step

and so does the door.

Everything on earth was made to be crossed over
                    then out.

There is no manual for memory
            —no place to put your hands.

Snowflakes freeze into hail to assault you properly
as the greying twilight slices through the earth,
bisecting you.

Do you feel that?
    In another time, someone is holding your hand.

Time was invented to give the mind something to hold.
(Dreams are the mind's way of communicating hunger.)

In Korea,
                old men are dying,
        and children are learning how to speak.

The days die first for others.

Tell me,
is it morning, where you are?

No. The night is eating its own tail.

Do you know where you are?
Yes. I am in the dark. Light refuses to touch me, still.

Still?
                    Still.

You used to be still, before I met you.

                    That sounds true.

Up ahead,
        smoke rises from the snow-blank page.

In winter, fire comes as a relief,
not a warning.

Smoke means someone lives here.
            Follow the trail of singed air.

    Look now,
your body is carving a snow trench,
hot breaths floating skyward,
where morning is in the fetal position,
waiting.

50 paces ahead—a door.

Also, forward.

The King of Grief

I have no interest in leaving a mark on the world.
The world has given me plenty and has earned
little gratitude for its effort.
Still, this ship has been leaking for years with
unpaid debts,
   loose eyelashes,
   and hand-made mugs
which had seemed a good idea at the time.

And yet.

They'll say I was a Renaissance Man,
except for that last part.
The smart-looking lawyer with the leather folder
will arrive at 9 o'clock to tell you precisely
what knowing me was worth.
   You see,
death is difficult to schedule
but the After Part is all industry.

A redistribution of matter.
If the universe made any sense,
King Solomon would have had it right.
Citing this, the lawyer in her thick frames
and pointed chin would take the pearl
necklace into her hands,
sever the bonds,
and give a pearl to each of you.
And each beloved friend
would take the pearl in the palm of their hand
and remember the ocean.

   'My,'
they would remark,
    'I remember this pearl when it belonged to the clam
    and I remember this pearl in the bucket on the ship
    and on the jeweler's workbench
    and dangling from her neck
    like a raindrop on the window.'
But this is impossible.
You dear ones only knew the necklace
and besides,
the lawyer would never.
She knows it is neither fair
nor practical
to be left with a fragment

of the whole.

And yet.

And yet.

Light Years

The walls of Ancient Athens
ran from the citadel to the sea.
It is entirely natural
to defend against the concept of cataclysm,
denying the crater as we crawl out of it.
Science insists upon a source, you know.
    "We'll have tea someday,"
I promised him,
    "And I will tell you everything."
Hand in impermanent hand,
he drifted towards the center of the universe
as the ocean bore me back.
It is a hard thing to lose
a Captain to the sea
and harder still to reject the surf.
    These days,
I am not on speaking terms with Astrophysics
or the orbits they support.
But if it truly is the fate of matter to be continually reborn,

the pearls of us perpetually restrung,
then tea time promises are possible
even if we are not ourselves,

but molecules commingling
in the same cup.

Deep August

The sun is also a mouth,
gaping
in the face
of all the light
it cannot bear.

Learn to hear
the nightly cricket hum as a
hymnal,
Listen for their chorus of
       'thank-you, thank-you, thank-you.'
Their evening song is sung from
lifeboats
for every day that
they make it to the end,
  unburnt.

In the evenings,
I mark the page

where the plot line strays.
Some days are empty like
me,
resounding with the echo of all I
abstain from.

In the absence of a glowing mouth,
a hymn
hums its way through a body
that is linen-tangled
yet still alive:

> Fear and longing go hand in hand
> while the ship of my fate is manned
> by a far too-impatient sailor,
> unaccustomed to the luxuries of
> land.

Your company provided a
   landing
away from which I have sailed
ever since the day
you called my soul
a ship
in want of
mending.

Again, it strikes me,
accompanied by a familiar ache,
that I've never feared love in its absence.

Only in its vast,
all-encompassing
    wake.

Συγγράφεια

I'm a walking shipwreck, baby. Timber cracked open like a rib cage beneath the flying fists of waves. Sometimes the future isn't supposed to happen. Sometimes it's just history and memory and your voice not asking me to stay. White flags and brine. *Is it ten, or is it nine?* Pirates steal everything of value but leave the grief. (Make sure to leave a light on so they can see the house is empty.) It's hard to destroy yourself so it's best to do it by accident. Close your eyes. Catch a train. Leave a note. Withstand the night. See the light over the ocean and mistake it for a sign. Lord it's hard to see through the smoke when you're raining hail and fire—please try to be subtler, next time. The ocean floor is so so soft and I'm clutching the emeralds to my chest as you tell me: *You bleed like the rest of us, so hurry up already.* You paint your nails like you're readying for war, and I could have sworn you knew the future and I was right. I was right.

Where Life Dwells

I once saw the curved branch
of a yellow birch tree
and mistook it for an owl.
I waited by the roadside for the owl to lift its head
but it never did.

Parts of my life have been devoted to empty branches
where I thought life dwelled.

Plato Longs for Us

Get in here! The show is starting soon.
The one in which we convert mirrors into windows
and old bones into suitcases.
Let the haberdashers open their doors
to feather the world.
Tell the velvet thunderclouds to come as well;
there is no praise for holding in the roar.
They don't teach you this in school,
but it is very important when you fall down the stairs
to hit every one on the way down. No skipped steps.
One must approach life thoroughly.
But who am I to proselytize?
    Sincerity is a hell of a drug but
    no one at this party wants in on my line.
It's good to pace—to underline your thoughts as they fall
    from the cave.
    (Plato dreams of shadows so real!)
Light slices through the trees like cake.

I'm no expert but this might mean
that I'm awake.

Dry Kindling

Not in a dream but after the dawn
I thought of you. I heard you yawn.
You would have laughed at the notion
of the small service held in a room
with no windows that still insisted upon curtains.
Reality has been heavy-handed lately—
metaphors without the dignity of verses.
I came home to wash my face
with "Take it Away" makeup remover.
Go figure.
At the end of the drive sits a cardboard box.
It reads:
dry kindling.
(Pyromaniacs everywhere rejoice.)

   Why am I still talking?
Someone else should speak.
Did I ever tell you about the *Other World?*
The one in which we grew from the dirt

with our wide, sunflower faces,
arching towards the light?
It is kinder there,
where we drink in the dawn with our whole faces
and night doesn't trouble us
because it never comes.
And if it did, *who would believe it?*
Us, with our sun-streaked cheeks
and endless conversation?

And what would we say to the arrival of the darkness?
What took you so long, perhaps.

Aeneas

Dear Universe: Please do me the curtesy
of binding my wrists to the tracks yourself.
It is too much to expect me
to make the conscious choice.
My shoulders ache beneath the weight I fail to carry.

BUT YOU WILL FOUND A CITY.

Yes, but I will have to build the city.

BUT THE CITY WILL STAND FOR A THOUSAND
YEARS.

I am hungry. I am mad with it.

THE CITY SHALL PROVIDE SUSTENANCE.

But my hunger is for the absent.

THE CITY SHALL PROVIDE SHELTER.

For the absent?

For the absent?

Craters

I will tell you now of the important things:

Of threadbare cardigans, slanted sunbeams, carved moon craters, well-read newspapers, and blue-black spectacles. The way he underlined my name by saying it. The gravity of presence. Lighthouses as small as candles. So much light in the kitchen but not enough to show the way. "He is at sea," they said, putting their faith in voyages – in perpetual becoming. He is at sea and will forget us soon. He shall drop anchor only when there is no one to miss. The star-crusted sky bursting with infinity, he will close his eyes and remember he had a mother. He will open them and remember he had been a father. His ship is made from waves, like with like. A star will fall from the heavens, and he will recognize it as a heart. Mine.

Anchises

Come with me.

> Where?

I don't know, yet.

> Are you searching for something?

Yes.

> What?

A home where we both could live.

> What about this one?

It's on fire.

> Who lit it?

Other people.

> Always other people...

Are you coming?

> I can't walk.

I'll carry you.

> I'm too heavy.

No, you're not.

> Know your limitations, boy.

I have none.

        You have so many; sometimes, they're all I see.

I know.

                               You're getting tired.

I know.

May

Hey.

    Can you hear me?

    Sometimes I think you keep me around

    just to make your shadow l o n g er.

    On the nightstand,

    a photograph masquerading as a bookmark.

    I read the last line first,

    every time.

    Unfortunately,

    I love the same way.

I once met an angel in an art gallery.

    "I hate to break it to you,"

    she said,

    "But there's nothing more punk rock

    than staying alive."

I liked you better as an idea than a person.
   Sorry.
   I know, I know.
   I used to be a dog
   but now I'm just a bitch.
   Call it inspiration.
   Call it 'catch you later.'

There's no nice way to say this
but I think you might have been a meteor shower.
Broken open over me,
bleeding out like wine—
a good vintage for a bad year.

Life is a question
which you answer by
moving.

Hey!
I knock against my skull.
Are you still in there?

Because in the end
it doesn't matter how good the story was.
   Ships at the bottom of the sea
   know enough to stay that way.

Farewell

So I'll take a little time,
mark it out in my mind,
and sing it back to you.

My friend,
I do believe
this is the end
but never mind.
It is a half-forgotten fact.

I do believe in bigger things.

Part II

«L'angoscia che tu hai
Forse ti tira fuor de la mia mente,
Sì che non par ch'i' ti vedessi mai».

"Perhaps the anguish you endure
Has cast you from my memory, for it seems
I've never looked upon your face before."

- *Inferno*, Canto IV, trans. Anthony Esolen, lines 43-45

Lessons in Optometry

Here are some things you ought to know about me:
My favorite word is 'tragic,' and someday
I'll know why.
I tend to measure my life in diametric benchmarks
to see how far from belonging I can get.
Think of me as a scientist calculating
light-years—how fast my glow can reach your eyes.
Am I making any sense?

That was Option 1.
Let me know if Option #2 is any clearer.
  Can you see me now?
Days pass. Clouds glide over. We are permitted
to suffer but we must hope.
Lately, I've been feeling like I don't belong
on this planet, which is really inconvenient
due to scheduling reasons.

Sidenote:

The words 'kinship' and 'kingship' are far too close together

    for either one to be taken very seriously.

For Option #3,

I suggest we take the middle ground, you and I.

We ought to circle our wagons and pitch a tent there.

Stars tend to burn their brightest

when they have no other choice,

and the view from No Man's Land is unparalleled.

Like the view from a spacecraft, removed from earth

but not deprived of air.

And I rarely forget but I can't remember

why I'm holding onto this knife

or who gave it to me

or what exactly

I'm meant to cut away.

No, I will not be outsourcing my dignity today.

Rage and kindness can dine together in the same house

and if I am the thing haunting it,

then darling, my widow-face will break them both.

    Can you see the green light? Try squinting a little harder.

I recognize that it is always better to dance *with* your feel-
   ings,
than around them.
Only the insatiable can ever be satisfied to hope
and I suppose that means this hunger knows
where it's headed.
At the end of the day,
I long to sit you down,
hand you my identity papers,
and show you who I am.
But this is impossible.
Who I am is three years away,
laughing in an Irish pub.
But that tiny little soul is still in here,
beyond the tragic mile-markers, beneath a covered wagon,
brimming with light, singing Queen songs to a knife that
   isn't mine,
face full of dignity and hunger
beneath this avalanche of selfhood.

   I take this poem and affix it to the wall in front of you.

Can you see me now?

Futures

They say that years double as lessons—
educations in blessings and deficiencies.
I fetch a pen to list the joys, instead:

1)   The way light cups the face of the world before
     breaking over it. The city lights catching in her hair.
     How sunlight scatters over the bed in fractals, then waits
     while the girl makes toast like it's her job. *Lux fiam.* Let
     me be light.

2)   How, when he awoke with one and a half legs, I dreamt
     him back to standing. A gentle fiction. I close a book and
     open a window. Each time I end a sentence, I glimpse
     completion. When you forget my name, I do as well. But
     today is a good day, I can tell. The answer isn't in the
     leaves, but in leaving.

3)   It might be the wine talking, but tonight, the timeline
is cracked open. The future speaks a foreign language
but still, I can hear it. There is a life there, as well as
enough tomorrows to stack atop one another, creating
something tangible. A foothold. Hope lives in the steps
after this one.

Why?
Because my life didn't end in the hospital waiting room.
Because
the years are falling from my eyes like anchors whenever I
enter a room.
The black cat that resides in my chest has a name.
It isn't mine, so why do I care for it?
Why do I tend to the ache like a garden, making it feel
comfortable?"
Safe?
These ribs are not pillows on which to rest
nor are they shutters to keep out the cold.
(I used to be cold before I met you.)
The days pass around me as I am learning how to feel safe
in this skin.

Because I am loved by this ache in me.
Why else would it keep coming back?

Even at night,

I do not go to bed empty handed.

The library of my heart is cluttered with memory.

In the next life, I should like to be a minimalist.

A careless soul that takes nothing with it.

Because singing in the car on the way home from the
    restaurant

is a lesson in taking up space in the universe.

I want to take up space.

A gentle sort of 'take'—nothing stolen.

My hands are up; they're always up.

Eyes up

to where dawn is remembering itself.

Morning is here.

I am so much more than I've been called.

Mhàbu

Boot prints braiding over the hill.
The mind, clearing, as in a forest.
The bent spine of this
horse-shoed college,
all hollowed-out against the mountainside,
is battered nightly with rain and winds.
I used to think that mountains
were burial mounds for gods
but now I think they might be pillows.
Not everything is in need of burial—
just lay your head down.
And if there is some ancient spirit
curled beneath the earth, let it rest.
Exhumation is unnecessary.
They say that grief is corrosive;
if you don't give it a name,
it will assign one to you.
    Well then,
    call me *Mountain Side.*

call me *New Wind*.

Call me from the Mainland

when you need to hear my voice again.

Mantra

I do not wander aimlessly
through the unfeeling wilderness.
I am only in a forest,
carving a new path.
The others will join me here eventually.

   This darkness that knows me
   allows me to savor the light.
   The most necessary paths
   are taken at night.

While we're at it,
I will not do violence to myself
by stifling my essence.
If the world is harsh,
I will not respond
by rolling up my sleeves
and adding to its rotten work.

Miasma

There is a bathtub in the kitchen.
It is clawfoot, pearl-colored, and pristine.
Shostakovich plays from the other room
as I crouch before it
on my knees,
not repenting, but peeling
the vegetables over it.
Turnips.
Carrots.
Potatoes.
Cucumber.
I strip them naked and dunk them in the bath.
A narrow bar of sunlight through the window
divides the room into *hers* and *mine*.
The flat is empty.
There is no one to notice as I lather
the vegetables in her rich body wash.
I take a carrot between my teeth
and it burns all the way down.

I wash and chop and toss the little heads

into the simmering pot.

The beaded cord snakes between my fingers,

soap bubbles parting,

then drowning,

as I fumble for the skins,

scraping them from the bottom of the tub.

Footsteps on the stairs.

A door opens.

'The girls and I will spend Christmas in Copenhagen,'

she says,

watching me scrape dead skin from the floor.

(It's a carrot in front of a dead horse.)

When I ask her whether this is enough for her to stay

she takes the bottle of soap

and drinks it.

No.

It isn't.

Haiku #2

Chaos is chronic;
it requires us to have
a united front.

Exit Stage Right Pursued by the Horrors of Being Alive

I have it on good authority that this season
will end. Even living on the outskirts
I still have neighbors and they tell me

how the light from my yard spills into theirs
just to tickle the apple blossoms.
In Mhàbu, a woman in town told me about the time

she came upon a dead sheep.
When her husband refused to touch it,
she tied her hair back and became a shepherd of the After.

She sheared the wool, carded it, and made a blanket.
Now, the sheep lies naked in the brush
while the children doze beneath its coat.

All of this to say,
if a creature can keep others warm in death
imagine how much you can do while you're alive.

Gabriel

If Autumn is the most beautiful death,
then winter is its haunting.
A ghostly period on which

    to

           hang

                  bows,

the decorative corpses
of a different season.

July and August are dead
—you killed them.
You light a cigarette beneath a
streetlamp, knowing this.
Two lights,
though unequal,
flicker on the edge of dawn.

What separates angels from ghosts is beauty;
to be haunted is to be cared for in reverse.

To feel so loved by an absence
that you fear it.

In a dream, I tell you this:

That on our knees we beg for angels,
while ghosts come to us
willingly.

Angels are beautiful because we cannot touch them.
Ghosts are hideous because they can touch us,
and they do.

Above us,
the lamplight flickers out.

  [God is blinking.]

The difference between ghosts and angels is beauty.
A dying man thinks Gabriel is gorgeous,
but a dead man thinks the beauty lies with us.
That's why they cannot look away—
    the ghosts.
They miss the way our bones
are hidden on the insides of ourselves,
still awaiting burial.

And history,
you mutter beneath your smoking hand.
   Ghosts have a history,
   but angels do not need to.
   Perfection cannot bear to have a past.

I'm always forgetting that part.

The part about time becoming us.

Lethe

I.
Floating lilies. Steam off the water.
An entire village out searching for its daughter.

   The river Lethe swells over my bed;
   everyone dreams this dream
   before they're dead.

II.
There's a girl standing in the yard.
She says her name is Time.

III.
Heroes are wingless.
they do not leave
so much as they become.

   Did no one tell you that
   departure is tantamount to violence?

IV.

There's a girl standing alone in the yard.
She says her name is Mine.

V.

Ancient Greek states the matter clearly.
When a Greek man says 'Μου λείπεις,'
he means:
'You are absent from me.'
　　The problem lies with you.

I used to think that no matter what
direction you started off in,
you would end up at your own door.
Now that you've left me,
I'm not so sure.

All I feel is absence.

VI.

I don't know how much longer I can run
without you chasing me.

VII.

I ought to have been stronger,

and better than I was.
More daring.
Instead, I am here,
mistaking streetlights for lighthouses
and missing you greatly.

VIII.
The poet covers
my eyes with his hands.

Perhaps that is why you are so disturbed,
my boy—
you are holding onto the light
of dead stars and pretending that
they have not died.

Ithaca

I want to leave you with something,
    the mother says.
A feeling that swallows every other one,
lovingly.

She chops her lettuce on the table,
beheading it.
    A mother
    is anyone who looks for you.

Odysseus could have come home sooner.
The hearths were more than ready,
    Penelope's hand in the doorway,
    doubling as the ground beneath his feet.

    Come home to Ithaca.
    Odysseus, come home.

The mother turns on the stove
   and tosses in the broken heads,
   weeping for none of them.

   I want to leave you with something,
   she repeats.

   And though you don't know why,
   little 'sorrys' fill your mouth like wine.

Dinner isn't ready yet.
Don't spoil it by swallowing the silence
   down
   & down
   & down.

   Silences
   are their own alphabet.
   In classical music,
   the un-played note is also a choice.

The mother
   is asking you to come home
   even as you pass her the salt,
   still trailing three years behind.

Tied to a mast,
you peel the carrots
   to shield yourself
   as the black-seed sirens chant:
   Welcome home,
   Welcome home,
   Come home,
   among the rocky breakers.

You will have many homes
before you're done
   and most
   will be made of paper.

You will knock on doors
with bread in your hands
   —an offering.
And when a man answers,
   you will ask him to
   tell you your name
   in a language you can
   understand.

Inside your body
lies the potential for violence

—your task is to beg your own forgiveness.

A hand extends,
but some people
   can only love through windows,
   or gloves,
   their breaths fogging the glass
   they do not dare to breech.

   Come home,
   the mother says,
   this time in words.

"Dinner is ready."

I. Untranslatable

My soul was written on papyrus scrolls
no one could decipher.
Written half in pictures,
half in song,
their language
lost along the way.

So I waited in my wreckage
for a historian to say:

'I've known this meaning all my life—
How I wish I'd found you sooner.'

II. Unübersetzbar

Meine Seele war auf Papyrus Schriftrollen
niedergeschrieben,
die niemand entziffern konnte.
Geschrieben zur Hälfte in Liedern,
ihre Sprache
auf dem Weg verloren.

Also wartete ich in meinen Trümmern
auf eine Historikerin, die sagen würde:

‚Ich habe diesen Sinn schon mein ganzes Leben ver-
standen—
Wie ich wünschte, ich hätte dich eher gefunden.‘

Hearth

Love! Love! Love! The little bell tolls
and I think I might be living in a clocktower
or a convent where bells ring upon the hour
and on Sundays and on holidays even when you forget
and especially when you forget
and somehow I've forgotten to lock the door
behind me when I came in from the rain
but it doesn't matter now because I'm dry
and we're both sitting by the fire that doesn't burn
anything but just lights the room.

Canto II

It is too late in the day

to pretend we speak the same

dead language.

All around us,

dinosaur bones are poking out of the dirt.

They have teeth large enough to kill us

but no follow through.

    Tell me,

is love always this terrible,

or are we doing it wrong?

I collect your words from

where you've placed them down

in the dust, and feast

on the half-eaten syllables.

There is no sound a deer can make

that its mother does not know.

To forge a language,

then,

is to be monstrous enough

   to have to name it.

In Florence,

deals are done only

in an epigonic tongue.

There are manuscripts in my study

that are all

   begat,

   begat,

   begat,

and if God's work

is one long tapestry of souls joined

together by a single thread,

then I am pierced by an eternity

that goes forth,

as do we,

peopling the earth

with our little agonies.

Allor si mosse, e io li tenni dietro.

   He set on, and I held my pace behind.[1]

Wolves and lions aside,

there are enough questions in my heart

that I would distrust any god

claiming to know the answers.

  As often as I long for a savior,

I wish more fervently

---

1. Dante, *Inferno*, trans. Anthony Esolen (NY: Modern
   Library, 2005), 1.136.

to be left among my native tongue

of ruin.

　If the fall was mine—

　if my insides are nothing more

　than brimstone and bone—

then all this darkness I've created,

I also belong to.

Nothing is outside belonging,

at least.

Fugue

They say that nothing on earth is fatherless;
everyone must have something to think about at night.

White-knuckled,
I swerve around the roadkill like a Catholic
pretending not to see the steeple—
as though every broken thing
was put there by other people.

I'm sorry
you were a pitcher we drank from, endlessly.

I'm sorry the ocean took everything worth having.
I'm sorry the saltwater ate at your eyes
and that I didn't carry you
   and that there wasn't a place
   for you to be carried to.

      Troy, Rome, Ithaca—all this talk of refuge is

killing us.

There are some nights
I wish the gods were real.
   I'd settle for just one,
     no need in sending the full arsenal.

     'Like painters, ghosts are masters of negative space,'
               you said,
           then proved it.

I saw my first ghost when I was six.
In a bed of glass,
she brushed her hair
and watched me watch.

Impermanence turns me inside out.

Remnants

The last echoes of the Big Bang
were concealed between the syllables
of my wife's lilting laughter
to remind me that destruction
is always possible.
Sometimes,
we even build lives upon it.

   Creusa
used to apply her oil by candlelight.
Now, her face is a candle.
Her body, too.
The house went up in seconds.

Miles and miles and light years away,
the stars school the universe
on how to burn without blinding.
(Night lights, not torches.)

We need a new language for this,
I told him.
His weight was heavy on my back.

We are making one,
he answered me.
We used to play hide-and-seek in the garden,
my father and I.
I would climb the chestnut tree
and he would climb up after me,
complaining of its height.
    I wanted to be so high
        nothing on earth could touch me
apart from his hand.

I once asked him
why he climbed at all;
that old man
so afraid of falling.
Amo tē, he replied.
I love you,
so, I shall come to you
wherever you are.
    Wherever you are,
                I shall come to you.

Then one day,
he didn't.

Neither did I.

Stella

There is only one thing on Earth
of which I am absolutely certain:

That the stars may wander but always return,
and that we shall do the same.

Sleeping on My Best Friend's Couch

The night
dislocates its jaw
to hold me in its mouth.
Little sparrows
are lacing over the earth between the metal tracks,
not far from Union
but far enough for me.

   Do the sparrows know?
   Do they know about the tracks?
   Do they keep away from the metal
   because they know the way it shakes?

Even worse:

Do little birds
look at every straight line
we humans have placed as threats?

An oncoming doom?

I wonder where the sparrows go
when all is said and done.
I wonder if the sparrows know
of all the times the fury won.

A Reason

In all beauty there is reason,
not in the petals of the rose,
but in the tenacity of its stem.

    For stand,
    we must.

Connoisseurs of Lightness

I have a sneaking suspicion that the gods only invented
   Autumn
to demonstrate the concept of unrequitedness.

                      Note: The eulogy of a curtain-call.
             A vessel by which to smuggle grace into the world.

I'm tired of placebos.
Give me the real thing, Doc.
Jumper cables to the heart in the form
of a thunderstorm. Or a great wind
as it dances through a wheatfield.

                My throat is scraped raw from trying to sing
                         all this darkness out of me.

Change doesn't care about consent these days.

    Evolution is five drinks deep and indifferent to denial.

To be a human being is to chair your own trial.

'Life is long and suffering is inevitable,
a friend tells me,
but so is the joy.'

To be a connoisseur of lightness
is to realize that it is possible to be
complete and unfinished simultaneously.

You find yourself missing the world?

Come back to it, then.

Though this life may be restless, it has wings.
What a splendid catastrophe
I hope to make of things.

Forward March

I once asked a grave keeper what time it was.
He replied: *Not yours.*
Unfortunately,
I only participate in hope
when it's a group project.

There is a nonzero chance that insanity
is only unprocessed innovation.
I trudge through thickening snow,
crunching the numbers.

   [You must learn to romanticize your life a little,
    otherwise, your bones will start to poke through.]

Sometimes,
there's so much goodness in my mouth
I can hardly stand it.

Scraps from ESL Class

Min

It happened in Thursday.

I was still in pain.

Sun is brighter today.

Jiwon

English is the most difficult study.

We set blanket on the table.

It is cold today.

We should find a nice and quiet place.

Daniel

Yes, I go outside.

I was feeling dreams

will be true.

I am ready to introduce my house.

Bella

It was not totally a mistake

but a kind of it.

They need to make the world

better place.

It is time for eating dinner.

Henry

Sunrise in the beach

that I don't go in there.

New Year they little bit grow up.

Old.

I am older.

Geeyoon

Sometimes hard to solve the problem

or suggest some amazing idea.

Define scholastic.

Define fallacy.

Koma

I struggle my face

and all my body.

My address is her.

Define: agency.

It all depends on season.

Sun

I am so much up to my necks right now.
I died last Saturday.
(She was talking about her hair.)
When someone cross the line,
I put him on the other side of the border.

Milo

Teacher, I want to say to him:
Please use your words softly;
don't be aggressive.
It's hard to express that.

Yerim

I can't watch the cruel as I am
getting older.
Many limitation was cancelled.
I can hear wedding bells on my
friend's face—
she will get married soon.

John

Hoping is bored.

What is 'purchase?'

Is it happy?

Yes,

I'm think I'm happy.

Stella

I want to explore museum

or really, really large places

alone.

I think no questions.

It is finish.

More than a Warning

Like the prow of a ship
I live in a bed of salt.
This worn-out hope
doubles as a
locket with no picture inside it.
I feed it to the sea along with
                        all my foolish imaginings.

This good light
travelled through time to reach me—
    why should I greet it lying down?
Listen.
In the forest, or out at sea,
everything sings.
The prophets are always wrong,
you know,
about the cataclysm.
                        Everyone is quick to tell you
from whence it came.

I promise
I am more than a warning;
more than that blue-black sentinel
gazing down from the moors.
 My middle name is Unrequited,
 but I'm teaching myself
 to finish my sentences anyway.

I cannot tell you if I believe
in a gentle future,
but I believe in a future.

Let's name it afterward.

References

Alighieri, Dante. 2005. *Inferno*. Trans. Anthony Esolen. New York, NY: Modern Library.

Montreal Publishing Company publishes works of
poetry, drama, fiction, and non-fiction.
We seek writers that dare, and make us think—reconsider.
Relevance without fear.
Montreal Publishing Company
montrealpublishing.com